DISCOVER THE **MOST AMAZING WEAPONS AND WARFARE** ON EARTH!

MEGA BOOK OF
WEAPONS
& WARFARE

www.alligatorbooks.co.uk

© 2006 Alligator Books Limited

Published by
Alligator Books Limited
Gadd House, Arcadia Avenue
London N3 2JU

Printed in China

CONTENTS

WORLDWIDE WEAPONS

The way that wars are waged has changed unimaginably in the last one hundred years. The invention of steam power and petrol-driven engines were the first major developments in modern warfare. Where soldiers once fought on foot, soon they had speedy combat aircraft, mighty battle tanks and fleets of huge warships at their disposal. Modern bombs and missiles now strike their targets with pinpoint accuracy, while nuclear, biological and chemical weapons of mass destruction are an ever-present threat to international security. On the following pages you can read about some of the most powerful and deadly weapons in the world today.

NUCLEAR NATIONS

Our modern world is a much more complex place than it was during the Cold War, when the USA and the former Soviet Union were the only two countries with nuclear weapons. Today, nations like India, Iran, Iraq, North Korea and other nations may have developed the capability to launch long-range nuclear missiles.

How NATO Works

The North Atlantic Treaty Organisation (NATO) is an alliance of nations that work to implement the North Atlantic Treaty. This treaty grew out of concern about the strength of the Soviet Army in the years following World War II (1939–1945). In the event of any attack by the Soviet Union, European countries would have needed the help of the USA and Canada. The treaty states that if any of the member nations is attacked, all the nations signing the treaty will respond to the attack together.

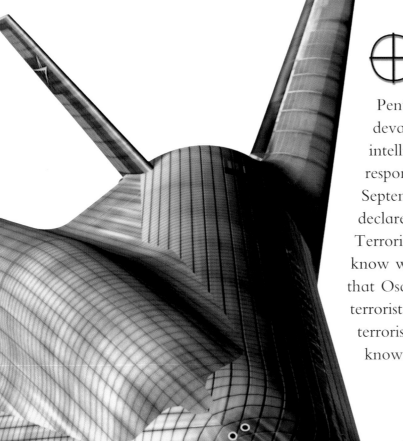

TERRORISM TODAY
The terrorist attacks on the World Trade Center and the Pentagon, on 11 September 2001, had a devastating effect on the USA. US intelligence cannot be certain who was responsible for the attacks. Soon after 11 September, President George W. Bush declared an international 'War Against Terrorism', but some Americans do not know who they are fighting. Most think that Osama bin Laden – leader of the terrorist group Al Qaeda – masterminded the terrorist attacks, but many other groups are known to be capable of such atrocities.

VENTURESTAR
The National Space and Aeronautics Administration (NASA) scrapped the 'VentureStar' X-33 space shuttle replacement in the late 1990s due to escalating costs, but the United States Air Force (USAF) continued testing for high-tech military applications.

COMBAT GUNS/INFANTRY WEAPONS

Guns have played a large part in warfare for hundreds of years. Pistols and rifles have long been popular with infantry soldiers. Artillery, cavalry and support troops also carry these weapons but mainly for self-protection rather than attack. The development of extremely powerful and deadly sub-machine guns and machine guns opened up a new frontier in the rapid advancement of weaponry. Today, these fully automatic weapons are used by armed forces throughout the world.

MEGA FACT
The first sub-machine gun to go into service was the Italian Villar Perosa, which was used in World War I (1914–1918). While sub-machine guns are not accurate over long ranges, they work well where intense, close-range firepower is needed.

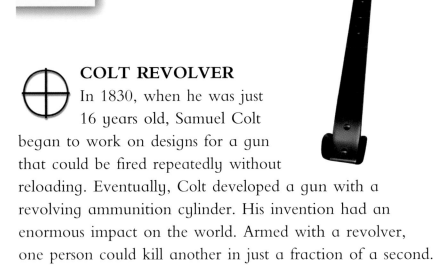

COLT REVOLVER

In 1830, when he was just 16 years old, Samuel Colt began to work on designs for a gun that could be fired repeatedly without reloading. Eventually, Colt developed a gun with a revolving ammunition cylinder. His invention had an enormous impact on the world. Armed with a revolver, one person could kill another in just a fraction of a second.

MEGA FACT
Machine guns were first mounted on helicopters in the 1960s. They are used to attack enemy infantry or as protection when flying into dangerous landing zones.

Gatling Gun/Vickers .303

Designed by Dr Richard Gatling, the hand-cranked Gatling gun first saw action in the American Civil War (1861–1865). It had between six and ten barrels and fired at a rate of 100 to 200 rounds per minute. The Gatling gun was later used by the US Army during the 1898 Spanish–American War.

The belt-fed British Vickers .303 inch machine gun was designed by the American engineer Hiram Maxim in 1891. This powerful and reliable gun played a vital role in policing Britain's vast colonial empire – involved in conflicts in India, South Africa and Sudan. It was withdrawn from service in 1963.

SIMPLE BUT EFFECTIVE

The machine gun is considered to be one of the most important warfare technologies of the past hundred years. These weapons have played an important part in every major conflict since World War I. Although they work on very basic concepts, machine guns are remarkable feats of precision engineering. The machine gun is capable of firing hundreds of rounds every minute, so it can mow down an entire unit of infantry soldiers in just a few passes. In response to the machine gun, military forces had to develop heavy-duty battle equipment, such as armoured vehicles, to withstand the powerful onslaught.

MAG

One of the best general-purpose machine guns (GPMGs) ever produced is the Mitrailleuse d'Appui Général or MAG. Produced in Belgium, the MAG was established during World War II and has become the most widely used infantry weapon of its type in the world. This extremely tough, reliable and accurate machine gun uses a conventional gas-operation system to fire NATO standard 7.62 mm cartridges.

The MAG can fire between 6,500 and 10,000 rounds per minute and can be used from a wide variety of mounts on aircraft, helicopters, ships and other vehicles.

MEGA FIRST
The first machine gun dates back to 1718, when Puckle's gun was developed in Britain. This early machine gun fired at a rate of seven rounds per minute.

MAUSER

Production of the Mauser Model 1896 'Broomhandle' automatic pistol started in 1896 and ended 43 years later. In that time, over one million pistols were produced. Also known as the C96 Mauser Military Pistol, this weapon was used as the standard-issue military side-arm of many of the world's major fighting forces. The C96 fired a 7.65 mm cartridge, 10-round box magazine loaded by stripper clip. The C96 saw more combat in the hands of the Chinese military than with any other nation.

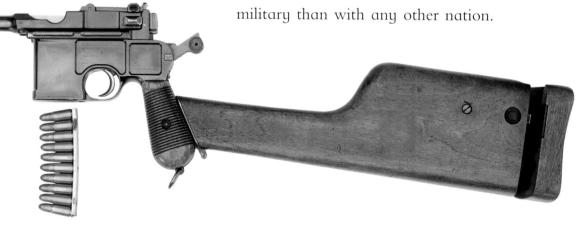

UZI

The Uzi was designed by the Israeli Uziel Gal more than 50 years ago. Although it is largely made from cheap pressed-steel parts, the Uzi remains one of the most effective sub-machine guns available. It has a firing range of around 200 metres and fires 600 rounds per minute. The magazine's location in the pistol grip makes it easier to reload in the dark. Police and military forces in over 20 countries still use this compact weapon, which first saw widespread action with the Israeli Army during the 1956 Suez–Sinai War.

AK-47

During World War II, most combat took place at close quarters. For this reason, weapons engineers in the Soviet Union produced the Avtomat Kalashnikova (AK-47) assault rifle in the late 1940s. Designed for battlefield ranges of less than 300 metres, this rifle is extremely reliable, easy to maintain and simple to use. The AK-47 is the most widely used weapon in the world, arming soldiers in over 100 countries. It has been a particularly suitable weapon for poorly trained soldiers in armies of the developing world, and it has also proved effective in guerrilla hands.

MEGA FACT
A machine gun fires long bursts over long ranges, spreading its bullets into a cone-shaped area called a 'beaten zone'. This area is one of the most dangerous on the battlefield.

REMINGTON 870

The Remington 870 was developed in the USA and has become one of the most widely manufactured shotguns of all time. The Remington 870 is a manual pump-action shotgun with a seven-round tubular magazine. It can fire a wide range of ammunition, from light-shot and riot rounds to heavy buck-shot. US Marine Corps personnel use the Remington 870 shotgun in boarding parties, as a security weapon aboard ship and as an embassy guard weapon with appropriate riot-control munitions.

MEGA REPEAT
In 1860, B. Tyler Henry, chief designer for Oliver Fisher Winchester's arms company, adapted a breech-loading rifle invented by Walter B. Hunt to create a new lever-action 'repeating rifle'. First known as the Henry, this weapon became better known as the Winchester.

DE LISLE CARBINE

Silent firearms have been used since the end of the 19th century. The British De Lisle Carbine was one of the earliest and most reliable silent commando weapons and possibly the quietest ever produced. Accurate to at least 250 metres, it had the ability to outrange almost all silent sub-machine guns and rifles.

Almost all De Lisle single-shot, bolt-action carbines were destroyed by British authorities at the end of World War II to prevent these powerful weapons falling into the wrong hands.

M30 Heavy Mortar

The US Army is one of the only armed forces in the developed world that still uses heavy mortars. These powerful weapons weigh over 305 kilograms, so they are difficult to move from place to place. The heavy mortars are mounted in armoured personnel carriers or fired from fixed positions. The M30 is a muzzle-loading, drop-fired weapon that can fire a range of ordnance, including high-energy (HE) shells, smoke, illumination, CS gas and chemical bombs. It has a maximum range of 6,800 metres with HE and 4,620 metres with smoke. Although the M30 is no longer in production, it remains the standard US Army heavy mortar.

MK 19 GRENADE LAUNCHER

The MK 19 automatic belt-fed grenade launcher is actually designated as a machine gun by the US military. This weapon first entered service in 1967 during the Vietnam War (1954–1975), and it proved to be very effective against personnel and light armour. When mounted on a tripod for infantry use, the MK 19 can deliver accurate fire at ranges up to a kilometre or more. The MK 19 can also be mounted on vehicles or in turrets and used with day, night and laser sights.

MEGA FAST

British troops are currently issued with the Enfield L85A1 rifle, which fires .22 inch rounds at 700 revolutions per minute set on automatic.

ANTI-TANK WEAPONS

Heavy-duty, powerful weapons are needed to destroy armoured vehicles as they blast their way through the battlefield. Shaped charge, short-range rocket and anti-tank guided weapons (ATGWs) have proved to be extremely effective for this purpose.

HOT

HOT is a long-range anti-tank weapon system that can be operated from a launcher or vehicle. Developed jointly by France and Germany, HOT is in service with 15 armies worldwide. It was used by Iraq during the Iran–Iraq War (1980–1988) and by Syrian forces during the conflict in Lebanon in the 1980s. HOT has a range of up to 4,000 metres and can penetrate 130 cm thick armour.

RBS-56 BILL

The Swedish Bofors RBS-56 – more commonly known as BILL – is the first human-portable missile designed to attack the top of tanks where the armour is thinner. The launcher of the missile is fitted with a thermal-imaging sight, which detects the heat generated by the engine of the armoured vehicle and uses it as a target.

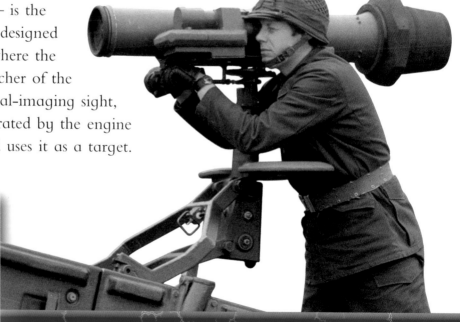

AT-4 Spigot

During the 1980s, the Soviet Union introduced a series of advanced ATGWs. One of these weapons – the human-portable Fagot – was designated AT-4 Spigot by NATO. The Spigot is a tube-launched, semi-automatic command-to-line-of-sight (SACLOS), anti-tank guided missile system equipped with a HEAT warhead. With a minimum range of just 70 metres, and a maximum range of 2,000 metres, missile speed is estimated at 185 metres per second, with a maximum flight time of 11 seconds.

POLYPHEM

The Polyphem fibre-optic guided missile is designed to strike long-range targets from light land vehicles and marine or land-based targets from the sea. In the latter case, the missile is launched from small warships or helicopters. Polyphem has a range up to 60 km and uses infra-red imaging for high-precision targeting by day and night against both mobile and stationary targets. France, Germany and Italy have recently secured a follow-on contract to continue the development of the Polyphem missile.

BGM-71 TOW

The Tube-launched, Optically-tracked, Wire-guided (TOW) ATGW is the most widely used of all the heavy anti-tank missiles. The basic missile consists of a shaped-charge warhead with a launch motor and a flight motor. Thermal and xenon beacons identify the missile in flight and help the operator steer it onto the target. TOW comes with a large warhead, which can defeat the armour of almost any kind of tank.

AIR-DEFENCE MISSILE SYSTEMS

Most of the world's major armed forces employ air-defence missile systems to counter enemy air attack. Many of these systems are extremely sophisticated. They can be deployed from vehicles, surface ships and helicopters or used in a portable mode. The firing units on these systems hold a number of missiles, all of which can be dispatched at airborne targets in a matter of seconds.

MISSILE POWER

Jernas is the export name for the Rapier FSC (Field Standard C) air-defence system. Jernas is based on the Rapier Mk 2 missile and launcher, which is in service with the British Army and Royal Air Force. Jernas provides defence against unpiloted aerial vehicles, cruise missiles and fixed and rotary-wing aircraft.

Torpedo

Robert Whitehead and Giovanni Lupis revolutionised maritime warfare in 1866 when they developed the self-propelled torpedo. Torpedoes are highly explosive underwater missiles. They make battleships and other large warships extremely vulnerable to attack by smaller vessels and submarines. In World War II, torpedoes were developed that could be launched from aircraft. Torpedoes with guidance systems and warheads are still deployed by submarines.

HIGH-TECH MISSILE

The Rapier missile is capable of engaging supersonic, low level, high manoeuvrability aircraft and can be towed behind medium-size vehicles and armoured personnel carriers (APCs). It is air-portable by transport aircraft or helicopter.

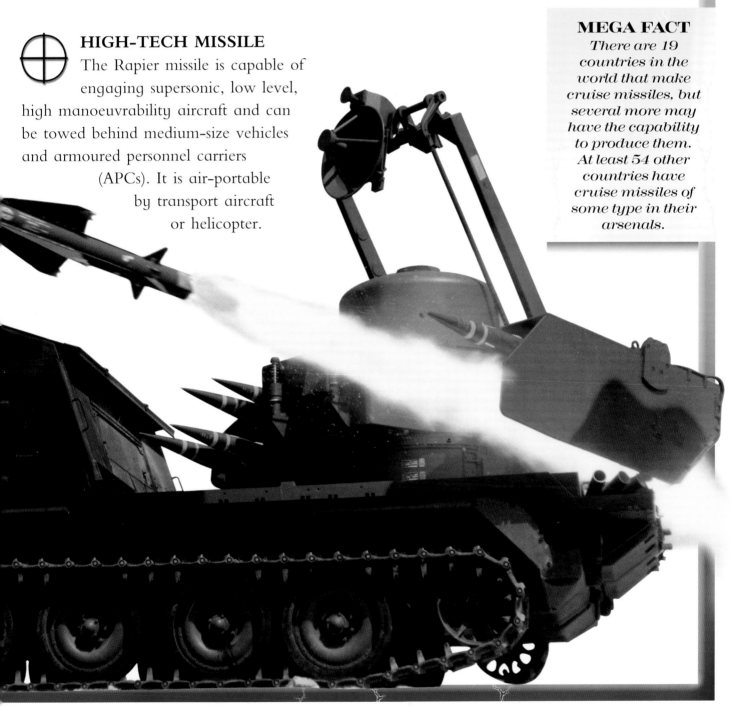

MEGA FACT
There are 19 countries in the world that make cruise missiles, but several more may have the capability to produce them. At least 54 other countries have cruise missiles of some type in their arsenals.

MISTRAL

Mistral is a very short-range air-defence missile system. Land-based vehicles, surface ships and helicopters are all used to deploy these missiles and a portable configuration also exists. Mistral entered series production in 1989. It is now deployed by 37 armed forces in 25 countries. Over 16,000 missiles have been ordered. The fully autonomous 'fire and forget' Mistral 2 missile is armed with a 3 kilogram high-explosive warhead loaded with tungsten bearing projectiles. The warheads come with a contact fuse, a laser-proximity fuse and a time-delay, self-destruct device.

MEGA FIRST

The Chinese invented gunpowder some time before 1000, and they were the first to use explosives in missiles. In the 1300s, the Chinese took another first when they successfully fired a multi-stage missile. By the 17th century western armed forces started to experiment with these 'war' rockets.

RAPIER

Each Rapier firing unit holds eight ready-to-fire missiles mounted on launcher rails on the walls of a rotatable turret. The Rapier Mk 2 missile is equipped with a fragmentation high-explosive warhead and comes with a multi-mode laser-proximity fuse. The propulsion system is a two-stage enhanced solid-propellant rocket motor. The Rapier entered service in 1996.

US AVENGER

The Avenger turret is mounted on a 4 x 4 High Mobility Multi-purpose Wheeled Vehicle (HMMWV), but it also operates on a number of other vehicles or in a stand-alone position. The Avenger was first deployed to support NATO troops during the 1991 Gulf War. The Avenger carries eight Stinger short-range air-defence missiles in two launch pods mounted either side of the turret.

MEGA FACT

Today's cruise missiles carry a warhead about the same size as one of a ballistic missile over a similar range. However, a cruise missile delivers the warhead with far greater accuracy and at a fraction of the cost of a ballistic missile.

UNPILOTED AERIAL VEHICLES

Unpiloted Aerial Vehicles (UAVs) are remotely piloted or self-piloted aircraft that carry a range of intelligence-gathering equipment, including cameras, sensors and other payloads. They have been used in a reconnaissance and surveillance role since the 1950s.

BREVEL

The Brevel is used for target location and general reconnaissance. The system comprises a command, control and communications vehicle, a launch vehicle with five to seven air vehicles, a recovery vehicle, a maintenance vehicle and a data-link terminal. The operational speed of each air vehicle is 150 km/h, the flight endurance is 6 hours and the operating range is 120 km.

HUNTER RQ-5A

The Hunter is a multi-role, short-range UAV in service with the US Army. It was developed to provide ground and maritime forces with real-time imagery intelligence at ranges of up to 200 km. The Hunter RQ-5A operates by day and night in a number of reconnaissance roles. Hunter UAVs have also been purchased by the Belgian and French armed forces.

GLOBAL HAWK

Global Hawk provides air force and joint battlefield commanders near real-time, high-resolution, intelligence, reconnaissance and surveillance imagery. This UAV is 13.4 metres long with a wing span of 35.3 metres. It can range as far as 22,200 km at an altitude of 19,812 metres, flying consistently at speeds approaching 640 km per hour for as long as 35 hours. Cruising at these high speeds and altitudes, Global Hawk can survey vast geographical areas with pinpoint accuracy. To demonstrate inter-operability between Australian and US military systems, Global Hawk flew 7,500 miles non-stop across the Pacific to Australia from 22 to 23 April 2001, setting a new world record for UAV endurance.

PREDATOR

The Predator system was designed to provide constant intelligence, reconnaissance and surveillance to strategic and tactical forces of the US military. Predator is composed of three parts: the air vehicle and associated sensors and communications gear, the ground control station (GCS) and the product- or data-dissemination system. Predator UAVs have been operational in Bosnia since 1995. Their intelligence-gathering capabilities have been exploited by NATO, the United Nations (UN) and US forces in over 600 missions.

MEGA FACT
Ground crew must unfold the wings of the Brevel UAV to launch the aircraft. An anti-icing system is incorporated into the wings for cold-weather operation.

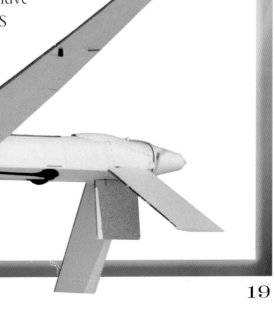

ROCKET SYSTEMS

The first people to use rockets as weapons were the ancient Chinese. They called them 'fire arrows'. British forces used rockets against France during the Napoleonic Wars (1799–1815). Rockets from World War II include the V-2, which had a range of 300 kilometres. Modern rockets include intercontinental guided missiles with nuclear warheads, air-to-air missiles (AAMs) and anti-tank missiles.

ROCKET RACE
Although torpedoes launched from ships, submarines or dropped from the air were effective anti-ship weapons during World War II, rockets took over, because they are much more effective weapons. Rockets can be launched from helicopters and ships.

MEGA FACT
Rockets use vast amounts of fuel to propel themselves and their payloads through space.

Landmines

One of the most deadly legacies of 20th-century warfare is the use of landmines. Most of these devices are found on or just below the surface of the ground. They are designed to explode when triggered by pressure or a tripwire. Since 1975, landmines have killed or maimed over 1 million people. Current estimates put at least 100 million live landmines in 70 countries throughout the world. This has led to co-ordinated international efforts to ban further landmine use and clear away existing devices.

NATIONAL MISSILE DEFENCE

A National Missile Defence (NMD) system has been the subject of much controversy in the USA for more than 50 years. According to its many supporters, the NMD system would provide a protective shield against a missile attack. In 1999, US Congress decided that enough talking had been done and passed a bill calling for the implementation of the NMD system to defend the USA from a growing number of countries developing long-range missile technologies. The United States plans to deploy the system within the next decade.

MEGA FACT
In 1903, Russian rocket engineer Konstantin Tsiolkovsky developed liquid-fuel rockets.

HIMARS

The High Mobility Artillery Rocket System (HIMARS) is a member of the Multiple Launch Rocket System (MLRS) family. Tests began in January 2002, when 12 MLRS M28 practice rockets were successfully fired from HIMARS to a range of 34 km. The main purpose of this rocket system is to engage and defeat air-defence concentrations, artillery, light armour, personnel carriers and trucks, but it also has a limited logistical and support role. HIMARS can launch the weapons and move away from the danger area at high speed before enemy forces can locate and attack the launch site.

Grad MLRS

Few systems in the artillery arsenal of the world's armed forces can boast such a wide spread as the Grad MLRS. The Grad rocket system was developed by the Soviet Union in 1963. Today, it is the main weapon in the inventory of armies in over 50 countries. In terms of its performance, the Grad MLRS is undoubtedly the best 122 mm multi-launch rocket system in the world. Modernisation has made it possible to raise the level of weapon functioning automation considerably, increasing the accuracy of the Grad MLRS at ranges of up to 40 km.

Alfred Nobel

Alfred Nobel was born in Stockholm on 21 October 1833. In 1859, Alfred and his father and younger brother started to experiment with an explosive liquid called nitroglycerin. In 1866, Alfred successfully mixed nitroglycerin with silica, which turned the liquid into a paste. Alfred found that he could mould the paste into shapes, which made the explosive safe for transportation. In 1867, Alfred patented the new material under the name 'dynamite'. Although Alfred believed his invention would have peaceful uses, dynamite became one of the primary means of war. Alfred left his estate to establish annual prizes in chemistry, literature, medicine, peace, physics, and physiology. The prizes are called Nobel Prizes in honour of this great businessman, chemist and entrepreneur.

URAGAN 9K57

The Uragan or Hurricane 9K57 is a 16-round 220 mm MLRS in service with the Russian Army. The launcher assembly is mounted on an 8 x 8 truck chassis. The launchers can rotate through 240 degrees and are arranged in two layers of six tubes with a layer of four tubes on the top. The maximum rate of fire is two rounds per second. The 9M27F rocket projectile fitted with the High Explosive Fragmentation warhead is designed to take out airfield runways, command posts, crossings, depots and other installations in addition to its anti-personnel role. The 9M59 rocket projectile is equipped with a cluster warhead fitted with anti-tank mines. In this way, the projectile can remotely lay mines in front of enemy combat units located in the battlefield and in concentrated areas.

MEGA FACT
Smerch is the long-distance missile of the MLRS world, with a maximum firing range of 90 km.

COMMUNICATIONS

The communication of tactics and positions is critical during military operations. Military units in the field rely on communications to report their positions and receive orders and other feedback from commanders back at headquarters. Some forms of communication, such as signal flags and smoke signals, date back hundreds of years, but modern communications are highly sophisticated.

FIELD RADIO

Unlike the first field radios, which required a wagon and team of horses to transport them, soldiers carry modern radios inside a back-pack. Many field radios have complex, built-in security systems, which makes it impossible to decode a message without the correct equipment. Most military radios operate in the very high frequency (VHF) range and in the high frequency (HF) range between 1 and 30MHz.

MEGA STARS
In 1931, Karl Guthe Jansky of Bell Telephone Laboratories discovered radio waves emanating from stars in space while tracking the source of electrical interference on telephone transmissions.

MEGA FACT
The telegraph allowed Morse messages to be sent over long distances for the first time during the American Civil War (1861–1865).

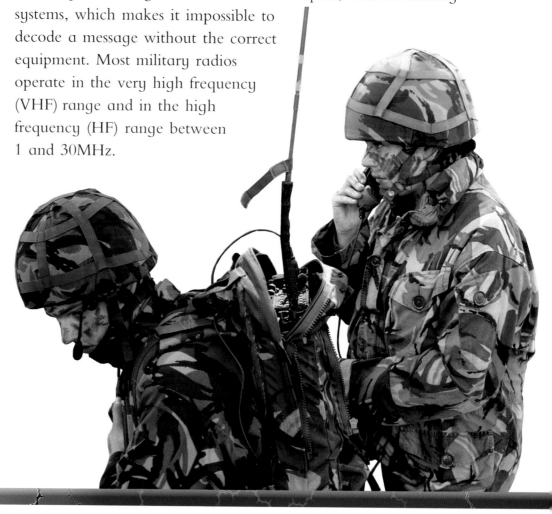

Morse Code

Samuel Morse devised the code that takes his name in 1850. It was used operationally for the first time during the Crimean War (1854–1856). Morse Code is an electromagnetic telegraph system that uses sequences of 'dots' and 'dashes' to represent the letters of the alphabet. Most messages were encoded before they were sent in case they were intercepted by the enemy. By the end of the World War I, most armed forces sent their orders by telegraph or wireless using Morse.

SATELLITE

The latest development in radio communications is the satellite. Satellites in space transmit and receive radio signals over vast distances, allowing messages from remote locations to reach almost anywhere in the world. Any object that orbits Earth is technically called a satellite. But the term is generally used to describe a useful object placed in orbit to perform a specific mission or task, such as communication satellites, scientific satellites and weather satellites.

ENIGMA

During the 1930s, the German military worked on a way of keeping military communications secret using cipher machines called Enigma. Enigma machines could encode messages in 150 trillion different ways! Before World War II broke out in 1939, Polish cipher experts passed on models and drawings of Enigma to British code breakers. British mathematician Alan Turing cracked the code a few years later.

DOOMSDAY WEAPONS

Unlike conventional explosives, nuclear, biological and chemical (NBC) weapons can be carried by the wind, spreading bacteria, biological viruses and radiation to far-reaching places. The fear that the Iraqi dictator Saddam Hussein was developing NBC weapons prompted a coalition force to invade Iraq in March 2003. The USA and Britain believed that Iraqi weapons of mass destruction could fall into the hands of terrorist organisations, with terrible consequences for the international community.

MEGA FACT

A biological weapon is packed with lethal bacteria or viruses or deadly toxins specifically aimed at killing or maiming as many people as possible. Agents in biological weapons considered to be the highest threat include anthrax, botulism, the plague and smallpox.

MISSILE MISSION

Harpoon missiles are used to sink enemy warships in an open-ocean environment. They provide the USAF and US Navy and Harpoon missile with a common missile for air, ship and submarine launches. The weapon system on this powerful missile uses mid-course guidance with a radar seeker to attack ships on the surface of the water.

The low-level, sea-skimming cruise trajectory, active radar guidance and warhead design of the Harpoon missile assure high survivability as well as great effectiveness. Other weapons, such as the Tomahawk missile, can be used against ships, but Harpoon and Penguin are the only ones used by the US military with anti-ship warfare as the primary objective.

Weapons of mass destruction

Compared to nuclear weapons, chemical and biological weapons are quite simple to make and cheap to produce. Working together in laboratories, scientists, physicians and engineers all over the world are able to produce these weapons of mass destruction. Chemical warfare is the intentional use of poisonous (toxic) substances. Biological agents are used to cause and spread disease. Although both kinds of weapons contain chemicals, micro-organisms or poisons, made by living organisms or synthetic process are used for biological warfare.

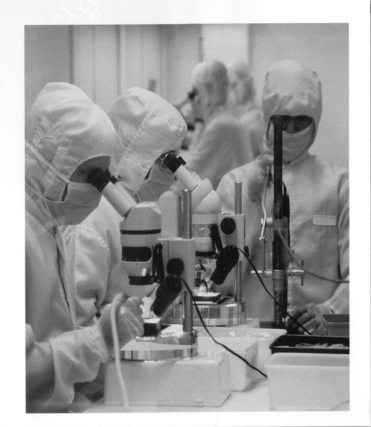

ATOMIC ATROCITY

In 1945, a team of scientists led by J. Robert Oppenheimer, Arthur H. Compton, Enrico Fermi and Léo Szilard detonated the first atomic bomb at the Los Alamos Laboratory near Santa Fé in New Mexico. Just a few months later, the USAF dropped two atomic bombs on Japan – one at Hiroshima and another at Nagasaki. These atomic bombs were responsible for the deaths of more than 100,000 Japanese people.

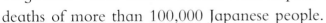

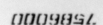

MEGA FACT
A chemical weapon is packed with lethal chemicals designed to kill or maim people. Chemical weapons fall into three main categories: nerve agents, blistering agents and choking agents.

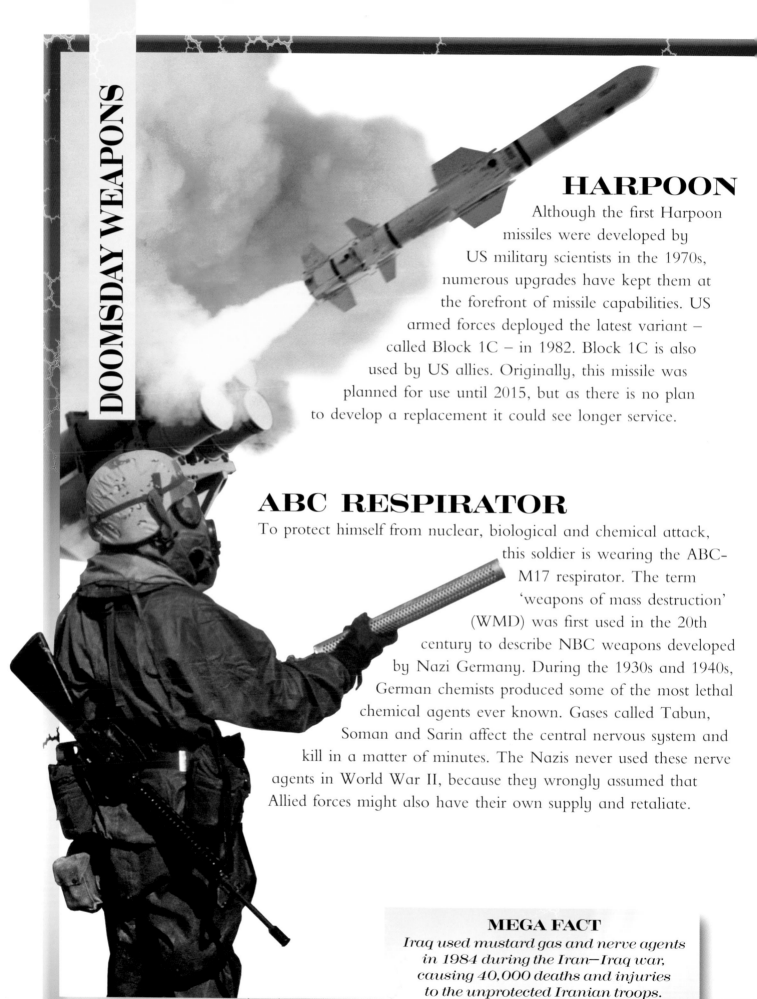

HARPOON

Although the first Harpoon missiles were developed by US military scientists in the 1970s, numerous upgrades have kept them at the forefront of missile capabilities. US armed forces deployed the latest variant – called Block 1C – in 1982. Block 1C is also used by US allies. Originally, this missile was planned for use until 2015, but as there is no plan to develop a replacement it could see longer service.

ABC RESPIRATOR

To protect himself from nuclear, biological and chemical attack, this soldier is wearing the ABC-M17 respirator. The term 'weapons of mass destruction' (WMD) was first used in the 20th century to describe NBC weapons developed by Nazi Germany. During the 1930s and 1940s, German chemists produced some of the most lethal chemical agents ever known. Gases called Tabun, Soman and Sarin affect the central nervous system and kill in a matter of minutes. The Nazis never used these nerve agents in World War II, because they wrongly assumed that Allied forces might also have their own supply and retaliate.

MEGA FACT
Iraq used mustard gas and nerve agents in 1984 during the Iran–Iraq war, causing 40,000 deaths and injuries to the unprotected Iranian troops.

Spy Satellites

The US National Reconnaissance Office (NRO) operates satellites for US intelligence services. US reconnaissance satellites, including the NRO's major equipment, are launched into Earth-orbit by the USAF. They are known by a variety of code names. These so-called 'spysats' include optical satellites with a large mirror to gather visible light for photography. Think of a Hubble Space Telescope pointing down at Earth taking secret pictures of terrorist organisations. Signals-intercept and detection satellites tune into radio, telephone and data transmissions. Ocean-observation satellites locate and determine the intent of ships at sea.

LITTLE BOY

'Little Boy' is the nickname given to the atomic bomb dropped on Hiroshima, in Japan, on 6 August 1945. A USAF B-29 bomber called 'Enola Gay' dropped the bomb, creating an explosion that generated a huge amount of deadly radiation. Little Boy caused devastating human injuries. Many people who survived the initial explosion died in the next few months. Many more died in subsequent years due to exposure of such high levels of radiation. Many of those that did survive developed genetic defects, which made them sterile or which resulted in the birth of malformed babies.

MEGA FACT
In 1942, a team working under Italian physicist Enrico Fermi at the University of Chicago produced the first controlled, self-sustaining nuclear chain reaction. This experiment and others resulted in the development of the atomic bomb.

AAA Anti-Aircraft Artillery

AAM Anti-Aircraft, or Air-to-Air, Missile. Missile carried by aircraft for air combat.

AFV Armoured Fighting Vehicle. APCs, tanks or any other vehicle protected by armour plate.

AGM Air-to-Ground Missile

APC Armoured Personnel Carrier. AFV designed to carry an infantry squad.

ARTILLERY Any large calibre cannons or guns for land use.

ATGW Anti-Tank Guided Weapon

BOLT ACTION Hand-operated firing action in which the user moves the bolt to load a shell into the breech (firing position).

BOMBER An aircraft fitted with external racks or internal bays to carry bombs for attacks on land or sea targets.

CBU Cluster bomb unit. Aircraft bomb that contains smaller bombs that scatter over a wide area.

MEGA FACT
In 1926, Robert H. Goddard, professor of physics at Clark University in Massachusetts, launched the first liquid-fuelled rocket up to 13 metres high.

GPMG General-Purpose Machine Gun. Gun that can be mounted on a tripod for long-range fire.

ICBM Intercontinental Ballistic Missile. Nuclear weapon that can travel long distances to hit remote targets.

IRBM Intermediate-Range Ballistic Missile. Nuclear weapon with a shorter range than an ICBM.

LGB Laser-Guided Bomb

LGW Laser-Guided Weapon

LMG Light Machine Gun. Weapon found in an infantry squad or section.

NASA National Space and Aeronautics Administration

NATO North Atlantic Treaty Organisation

NBC Nuclear, Biological and Chemical weapons

PE Plastic Explosives. Semtex is a plastic explosive.

RAF Royal Air Force. British air force.

RECONNAISSANCE The act of finding out any information that will help in battle.

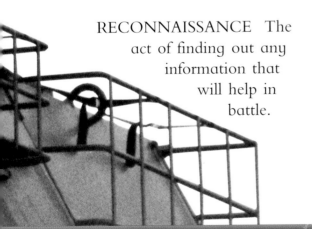

rpm Rounds Per Minute

SAM Surface-to-Air Missile. Lightweight AAM fired by one person from the shoulder or a long-range missile.

> **MEGA FACT**
> In 1996, the US Department of Defense admitted that at least 20,000 US soldiers may have been exposed to chemical agents during the 1991 Gulf War. The health problems many US soldiers faced may have resulted from the experimental vaccines provided prior to the conflict.

SATCOM SATellite COMmunications. Radio signals transmitted over huge distances via a satellite orbiting the Earth.

SACLOS Semi-Automatic Command-to-Line-Of-Sight

SMG Sub-Machine Gun

SP Gun Self-Propelled Gun. Artillery mounted on an AFV chassis to protect the crew and ensures their mobility.

SRAM Short-Range Attack Missile

SSM Surface-to-Surface Missile. Missile launched from the ground and aimed at another ground target.

TOW Tube-launched, Optically-tracked, Wire-guided

USAF United States Air Force

VSTOL Vertical/Short Takeoff and Landing

WMD Weapons of Mass Destruction

> **MEGA FACT**
> On 4 October 1952, Britain launched its first atomic bomb.

INDEX

Picture Credits

T=top; B=bottom; C=centre; R=right
Front cover (main), TRH; (TC inset), Reuters; (TCR inset), Jeremy Flack/API; back cover (main), TRH; (TC inset), Reuters; (TCR inset), Jeremy Flack/API; 4-5 (main), TRH; 5 (TR), Reuters; 6-7, TRH; 8 (T), TRH; 9 (B), TRH; 10 (T), Defence Picture Library; 10 (B) TRH; 11 (both), TRH; 12-13 (all), TRH; 16-17 (all), TRH; 18 (all), TRH; 19 (T), Reuters; 19 (B), TRH; 20-21, Reuters; 21 (TR), Jeremy Flack/API; 22 (T), Jeremy Flack/API; 22 (B), TRH; 23 (T), Hulton|Archive; 23 (B), Reuters; 24, TRH; 25 (T), Bettmann/Corbis ; 25 (C), TRH; 28 (B), TRH. All other pictures Alligator Books Limited.